ESSENTIAL
GUIDE TO SEASONS AND SAINTS

Libreria Editrice Vaticana

United States Conference of Catholic Bishops
Washington, DC

First printing, May 2013
ISBN 978-1-60137-124-9

CONTENTS

I. INTRODUCTION 1

II. THE PROPER OF TIME
(THE LITURGICAL SEASONS)................ 8

III. THE PROPER OF SAINTS 39

IV. SPECIAL OBSERVANCES.................... 127

V. CONCLUSION 132

ACKNOWLEDGMENTS......................... 134

I. INTRODUCTION

Christ yesterday and today
the Beginning and the End
the Alpha
and the Omega
All time belongs to him
and all the ages
To him be glory and power
through every age and for ever. Amen.

Blessing of the Paschal Candle, Roman Missal

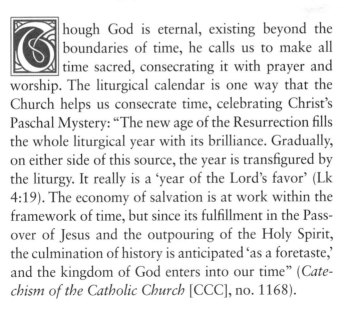hough God is eternal, existing beyond the boundaries of time, he calls us to make all time sacred, consecrating it with prayer and worship. The liturgical calendar is one way that the Church helps us consecrate time, celebrating Christ's Paschal Mystery: "The new age of the Resurrection fills the whole liturgical year with its brilliance. Gradually, on either side of this source, the year is transfigured by the liturgy. It really is a 'year of the Lord's favor' (Lk 4:19). The economy of salvation is at work within the framework of time, but since its fulfillment in the Passover of Jesus and the outpouring of the Holy Spirit, the culmination of history is anticipated 'as a foretaste,' and the kingdom of God enters into our time" (*Catechism of the Catholic Church* [CCC], no. 1168).

The first section of this book will consider basic elements of the liturgical calendar before turning to the seasons that make up the liturgical year, identifying the characteristics of each season that should inform liturgical planning and celebration. The third section will take a brief look at the saints celebrated in the General Roman Calendar including the *Proper Calendar for the Dioceses of the United States of America*. Finally, we'll look at some special observances associated with particular months and days.

SUNDAY

All liturgical time is centered on the celebration of Sunday, the Lord's Day. From its earliest days, recounted in the Acts of the Apostles, the Church gathered on Sundays to pray and to break bread in commemoration of the Lord's Resurrection. In fact, for centuries, Sunday was the only day on the liturgical calendar. No Easter, no Pentecost or Christmas. Just Sunday. Each Sunday was celebrated as Easter. As Pope John Paul II noted in his apostolic letter on Sunday, *Dies Domini* (*The Day of the Lord*), "Although the Lord's Day is rooted in the very work of creation and even more in the mystery of the biblical 'rest' of God, it is nonetheless to the Resurrection of Christ that we must look in order to understand fully the Lord's Day. This is what the Christian Sunday does, leading the faithful each week to ponder and live the event of Easter, true source of the world's salvation" (no. 19). As such, "Sunday must be considered the primordial feast day" (*Universal Norms on the Liturgical Year and General Roman Calendar* [*Norms*], no. 4). The celebration of Sunday begins on Saturday evening with the celebration of Evening Prayer I of the Liturgy of the Hours. Because the celebration of Sunday begins on Saturday evening, the Sunday Eucharistic liturgy may be celebrated then (see *Norms*, no. 3).

The faithful are obliged to participate in the Eucharistic liturgy each Sunday, unless prevented by some serious concern, such as illness. In addition to participation in the liturgy, the faithful should refrain from servile work, keeping the day free for prayer, reflection, relaxation, and time with family.

In some places, the Sunday celebration of the Eucharist is not possible due to the lack of priests. When the Eucharist cannot be celebrated on Sunday, in some instances, the local bishop may deem it advisable to permit Sunday celebrations in the absence of priest. Holy Communion may or may not be distributed during such celebrations. If such gatherings are not possible, the faithful are encouraged to gather as families or as other groups for prayer. In all cases, such celebrations should be clearly distinguished from the Eucharistic liturgy.

HOLY DAYS OF OBLIGATION

In addition to the Sunday observance, the Church sets aside particular days throughout the year on which the faithful are bound to attend Mass. One source explains this requirement: "Holy days of obligation are those important feasts of the Lord, Mary or the saints in the Roman Calendar that Catholics are morally obliged to observe by participating in the celebration of the Eucharist and abstaining from servile work" (*Holy Days in the United States: History, Theology, Celebration* [*Holy Days*], 7).

Prior to 1884, almost every U.S. diocese had its own calendar of holy days of obligation, often reflecting the various cultural roots (Spanish, French, English, etc.) of the region. The Third Plenary Council of Baltimore, convened in 1884, established a uniform national observance of six holy days of obligation. The Holy Father confirmed this decree in 1885.

Canon 1246 of the 1983 *Code of Canon Law* outlines the ten holy days to be observed in the Latin Church: Christmas, Epiphany, Ascension, the Body and Blood of Christ, Mary the Mother of God, the Immaculate Conception, the Assumption, St. Joseph, SS. Peter and Paul, and All Saints. The canon also permits conferences of bishops, with the approval of the Holy See, to suppress the obligation for some days or to move the observance to Sunday.

The bishops of the United States received the required approval to transfer the observance of Epiphany and the Body and Blood of Christ to a Sunday. The obligation to attend Mass on the Solemnities of St. Joseph and SS. Peter and Paul is not observed in the United States. These decisions left the United States with six holy days of obligation:

- The Immaculate Conception (December 8)
- Christmas (December 25)
- Mary the Mother of God (January 1)
- The Ascension (forty days after Easter)
- The Assumption (August 15)
- All Saints (November 1)

In more recent years, the United States Conference of Catholic Bishops (USCCB) has made two additional changes in the holy days of obligation, both with the approval of the Holy See. As of 1993, whenever the Solemnities of Mary the Mother of God, the Assumption, or All Saints fall on a Saturday or Monday, the obligation to attend Mass is suppressed. In

1999, the USCCB voted to permit the various ecclesiastical provinces of the United States to transfer the observance of the Solemnity of the Ascension to the Seventh Sunday of Easter. Two-thirds of the bishops of a given province must approve the decision to transfer this observance.[1]

TYPES OF OBSERVANCES

he liturgical calendar identifies four types of observances: solemnity, feast, and memorial, designated as either obligatory or optional (the designation of each observance is noted in the liturgical calendar given in Section III).

As the *Norms* note, "Solemnities are counted among the most important days, whose celebration begins with First Vespers (Evening Prayer I) on the preceding day. Some Solemnities are also endowed with their own Vigil Mass, which is to be used on the evening of the preceding day, if an evening Mass is celebrated" (*Norms*, no. 11).

---

1 Regarding the Ascension of the Lord, the ecclesiastical provinces of Boston, Hartford, New York, Newark, Omaha, and Philadelphia have retained its celebration on the proper Thursday, while all other provinces have transferred this solemnity to the Seventh Sunday of Easter.

The celebration of feasts is limited to the day itself, unless it falls on a Sunday in Ordinary Time or the Christmas season. In such cases, the feast will have a first Vespers, celebrated on Saturday evening (see *Norms*, no. 13). "Memorials are either obligatory or optional; their observance is integrated into the celebration of the occurring weekday. . . . Obligatory Memorials which fall on weekdays of Lent may only be celebrated as Optional Memorials. If several Optional Memorials are inscribed in the Calendar on the same day, only one may be celebrated, the others being omitted" (*Norms*, no. 14). Celebrants should take care in choosing optional memorials to ensure that celebrations of the saints do not overwhelm the Proper of Time.

Solemnities and feasts always have proper readings that must be used on these days. Some memorials have proper readings assigned as well. Unless proper readings are given, the readings assigned to memorials may replace the readings of the day. These readings are provided as options when it is appropriate to give added focus to the particular observance. Such choices should be made with care to ensure that the continuous reading of Scripture that marks the weekday Lectionary is not unduly interrupted.

II. The Proper of Time
(*The Liturgical Seasons*)

Advent

he liturgical year begins with the celebration of Advent. Advent begins four Sundays before Christmas (actually on the evening before) and concludes with the vigil Mass of Christmas. The *Norms* express the waiting time in this way:

> Advent has a twofold character, for it is a time of preparation for the Solemnities of Christmas, in which the First Coming of the Son of God to humanity is remembered, and likewise a time when, by remembrance of this, minds and hearts are led to look forward to Christ's Second Coming at the end of time. For these two reasons, Advent is a period of devout and expectant delight. (*Norms*, no. 39)

During the first weeks of Advent, the prayers and readings focus more specifically on preparing for Christ's second coming while acknowledging his presence among us even now. As Advent progresses, the focus turns toward preparation for the celebration of

the Nativity of the Lord. First, we look at the ministry of John the Baptist, proclaiming the coming of the Messiah. In the last days before Christmas (December 17-24), the readings offer immediate preparation for the Incarnation of Christ. These days are marked by praying the "O Antiphons," which herald the coming of Christ using ancient titles for the Messiah.

Though the secular world during this time focuses on decorating, shopping, and the anticipatory celebration of Christmas, the *Directory on Popular Piety and the Liturgy* notes that, for the Church, "Advent is

a time of waiting, conversion, and of hope. "Specifically, it describes these moments as, a

- "waiting-memory of the first, humble coming of the Lord in our mortal flesh; waiting-supplication for his final, glorious coming as Lord of History and universal Judge;
- "conversion, to which the Liturgy at this time often refers quoting the prophets, especially John the Baptist, 'Repent for the kingdom of heaven is at hand' (Mt 3:2);
- "joyful hope that the salvation already accomplished by Christ (see Rom 8:24-25) and the reality of grace in the world, will mature and reach their fullness, thereby granting us what is promised by faith, and 'we shall become like him for we shall see him as he really is'" (Jn 3:2) (*Directory on Popular Piety and the Liturgy* [*Directory*], no. 96).

O God, who wonderfully created the dignity
    of human nature
and still more wonderfully restored it,
grant, we pray,
that we may share in the divinity of Christ,
who humbled himself to share in our humanity.
Who lives and reigns with you in the unity
    of the Holy Spirit,
one God, for ever and ever.

(Collect, The Nativity of the Lord,
At the Mass During the Day, *Roman Missal*)

CHRISTMAS

n the evening of December 24, the Church begins its celebration of the Nativity of the Lord. "After the annual celebration of the Paschal Mystery, the Church has no more ancient custom than celebrating the memorial of the Nativity of the Lord and of his first manifestations" (*Norms*, no. 32).

Four Masses are assigned for the Solemnity of Christmas: a Vigil Mass, a Mass during the Night, a Mass at Dawn, and a Mass during the Day. In past centuries, the last three were known as the Mass of the Angels, the Mass of the Shepherds, and the Mass of the Incarnate Word, titles derived from the Gospels assigned to each liturgy.

O God, who on this day
revealed your Only Begotten Son to the nations
by the guidance of a star,
grant in your mercy
that we, who know you already by faith,
may be brought to behold the beauty of your
    sublime glory.
Through our Lord Jesus Christ, your Son,
who lives and reigns with you in the unity of the
    Holy Spirit,
one God, for ever and ever.

(Collect, The Epiphany of the Lord,
At the Mass During the Day, *Roman Missal*)

The celebration of Christmas does not end with these four Masses, however, for the most central mysteries' observances continue beyond a single celebration or day to allow time for extended reflection and celebration. While the secular world seems to want to conclude Christmas the next day, the Church is just beginning to celebrate. The celebration extends through the Octave (eight days) that concludes on January 1, and even beyond through the Feast of the Baptism of the Lord (see *Norms*, no. 12). The *Directory* describes the Church's continued celebration:

> During Christmastide, the Church celebrates the mystery of the Lord's manifestation: his humble birth in Bethlehem which was made known to the shepherds, the first of Israel to welcome the Savior; the Epiphany to the three wise men who had "come from the East" (Mt 2:1), the first of the Gentiles who recognized and adored Christ the Messiah in the child of Bethlehem; the theophany at the river Jordan in which the Father declares that Jesus is His "well-beloved Son" (Mt 3:17) at the outset of his messianic mission; the miracle of Cana in which Jesus "manifested his glory and his disciples believed in him" (Jn 2:11). (*Directory*, no. 106)

The days of the Christmas Octave include many special feasts. On December 26, we celebrate the Feast of St. Stephen, the first martyr, followed by the Feast of St. John, Apostle and Evangelist, on December 27. On December 28, we remember the Holy Innocents, the sons of Israel massacred by Herod in his futile effort to destroy the newborn King of the Jews. On the Sunday in the Octave,[2] we celebrate the Feast of the Holy Family of Jesus, Mary, and Joseph, honoring the human family in which Jesus grew to maturity, a model for our families as well. On the octave day itself, January 1, we celebrate Mary, the Mother of God, recalling "the divine, virginal and salvific motherhood of the Blessed Virgin Mary" (*Directory*, no. 107). The *Directory* also describes the final day, as a day to focus on the human need for peace:

> Since 1967, January 1 has been designated "world day for peace." Popular piety has not been oblivious to this initiative of the Holy See. In the light of the new born Prince of Peace, it reserves this day for intense prayer for peace, education towards peace and those values inextricably linked with it, such as liberty, fraternal solidarity, the dignity of the human person, respect for nature, the right to work, the sacredness of human life, and the denunciation of injustices which trouble the conscience of man and threaten peace. (*Directory*, no. 117)

2   When there is no Sunday in the Octave, the feast is transferred to the preceding Friday.

The Christmas season continues with the celebration of the Solemnity of the Epiphany, honoring the manifestation of Jesus as Messiah to the Magi from the East, a sign that Gentiles too are called into the unity of God's Kingdom. Though traditionally celebrated as the conclusion of the Twelve Days of Christmas, in the United States, this observance has been transferred to the Second Sunday of Christmas, meaning that it can be celebrated on any day between January 2 and January 8. The Christmas season concludes with the Feast of the Baptism of the Lord, when, through the descent of a dove, God made manifest that Jesus was his beloved Son, sent for the salvation of the world. When the Epiphany is celebrated on January 7 or 8, this feast is celebrated on the following Monday.

The observances of the Christmas season illuminate many key themes for the faithful:

- "the importance of the 'spirituality of gift,' which is proper to Christmas: 'a child is born for us, a son is *given* to us' (see Is 9:5), a gift expressing the infinite love of God, who 'so loved the world that he gave his only Son' (Jn 3:16);

- "the message of solidarity conveyed by the event of Christmas: solidarity with sinful man, for whom, in Christ, God became man 'for us men and for our salvation'; solidarity with the poor, because the Son of God 'who was rich but became poor for your sake, to make you rich out of your poverty' (2 Cor 8:9);

- "the sacredness of human life and the wonderful event that is every birth, since the Word of life came amongst men and was made visible through his birth of the Virgin Mary (see 1 Jn 1:2);
- "the messianic joy and peace to which man has aspired in every age: the Angels announce the birth of the Savior of the world to the shepherds, the 'Prince of Peace' (Is 9:5) and proclaim 'peace on earth to men of good will' (Lk 2:14);
- "the spirit of simplicity and poverty, humility and trust in God, suggested by the events surrounding the birth of Christ" (*Directory*, no. 108).

LENT

s the days of winter give way to spring in the Northern Hemisphere, the Church celebrates the season of Lent (the name "Lent" comes from the Old English word for "spring"). Like Advent, Lent is a season of preparation. As Advent prepares us to celebrate the Lord's Nativity, Lent prepares us to celebrate the Paschal Mystery of the Lord in the Triduum and Easter Season.

As the fathers of the Second Vatican Council intended,

> The Lenten season has a two-fold character: (1) it recalls baptism or prepares for it; (2) it stresses a penitential spirit. By these means especially, Lent readies the faithful for celebrating the paschal mystery after a period of closer attention to the Word of God, and more ardent prayer. . . .
>
> During Lent, penance should not only be internal and individual but also external and social. (*Constitution on the Sacred Liturgy*, nos. 109-110)

During this season, the faithful are called to focus on the traditional penitential practices of prayer, fasting, and almsgiving. These practices help to purify the mind and heart and help us recognize our dependence on God and our solidarity with our brothers and sisters who lack the basic necessities of life. In this way, these practices call us to renew our baptismal commitment to be conformed to Christ as members of his Body.

Lent is also the period of purification and enlightenment for those elected to receive the Sacraments of Initiation (Baptism, Confirmation, and Eucharist) at the Easter Vigil. Those who have never been baptized, having undergone a period of instruction and formation in Christian living called the catechumenate are called to the Sacraments of Initiation in the rite of election, typically celebrated by the diocesan bishop. The period of purification and enlightenment continues with the scrutinies, celebrated in the midst of the parish community. These rituals not only draw the elect toward the font and the Eucharistic table but rekindle in those already baptized a new commitment to their baptismal call.

The spirit of the Lenten season is expressed in liturgy and in popular piety. The Eucharistic liturgy is simpler. The *Gloria* is not sung (except on the two solemnities that often fall in Lent or at certain ritual Masses) and *Alleluia* is not used. Music and decoration are kept simple. More time is allowed for silence. Opportunities for reflection and to receive the Sacrament of Penance abound. Traditional devotions, particularly the Stations of the Cross, focus our attention on the sacrifice of Jesus who opened the gates of heaven for us.

Almighty ever-living God,
who as an example of humility for the human
*   race to follow*
caused our Savior to take flesh and submit to the Cross,
graciously grant that we may heed his lesson
*   of patient suffering*
and so merit a share in his Resurrection.
Who lives and reigns with you in the unity
*   of the Holy Spirit,*
one God, for ever and ever.

> (Collect, Palm Sunday of the Passion
> of the Lord, *Roman Missal*)

The final Sunday of Lent is Palm Sunday of the Lord's Passion. The liturgy begins with the blessing of palm branches and, in some cases, procession to the church. The Gospel of the day is the account of the Lord's Passion, focusing our attention on the fact that he was heralded as the Son of David and was condemned to crucifixion a few short days later. In this final week of Lent, called Holy Week, the Church celebrates the Chrism Mass. Traditionally, the Chrism Mass is celebrated on the morning of Holy Thursday. However, as is done in most dioceses in the United States, it is permitted to celebrate the Chrism Mass earlier in the week so that priests may return more easily to their parishes for the evening Masses. During the Chrism Mass, the bishop gathers with his priests, usually at the cathedral. The Chrism Mass includes the Renewal of Priestly Promises, the Blessing of the Oils of the Sick and of Catechumens, and the Consecration of Holy Chrism. Following the liturgy, representatives of each parish bring back to their parishes the oils that will be used in celebrating the sacraments in the coming year.

O God, who have called us to participate
in this most sacred Supper,
in which your Only Begotten Son,
when about to hand himself over to death,
entrusted to the Church a sacrifice new for all eternity,
the banquet of his love,
grant, we pray,
that we may draw from so great a mystery,
the fullness of charity and of life.
Through our Lord Jesus Christ, your Son,
who lives and reigns with you in the unity of the Holy Spirit,
one God, for ever and ever.

(Collect, Thursday of the
Lord's Supper, *Roman Missal*)

Triduum

he season of Lent ends at sunset on Holy Thursday. As Lent comes to an end, the Paschal Triduum begins. These "three days" (the literal meaning of Triduum), extending from sunset on Holy Thursday through sunset on Easter Sunday, are the heart and culmination of the entire liturgical year. In these days, we remember and celebrate ever more intensely Christ's Paschal Mystery, "since Christ accomplished his work of human redemption and of the perfect glorification of God principally through his Paschal Mystery, in which by dying he has destroyed our death, and by rising restored our life" (*Norms*, no. 18).

The first liturgy of the Sacred Triduum is the Mass of the Lord's Supper, celebrated on the evening of Holy Thursday. This Mass celebrates the institution of the Eucharist, the institution of the priesthood, and Christ's giving of the new commandment ("Love one another as I have loved you" [Jn 13:34]). After the homily, the celebrant may follow the example of Jesus and wash the feet of selected men. Traditionally, the gifts brought forward during the Preparation of the Gifts include gifts for the poor as well as the bread and wine needed for the Eucharist. After the people have received Holy Communion, under both kinds if the bishop permits, the Mass does not conclude with the usual Blessing and Dismissal. Instead, the celebrant, ministers, and all the faithful join in processing the reserved Eucharist to an Altar of Reposition where the faithful may watch prayerfully until midnight.

On Good Friday, Mass may not be celebrated in accordance with the ancient tradition of the Church. No sacraments may be celebrated except Penance and Anointing of the Sick. Instead, the liturgy of the day is the Celebration of the Lord's Passion. This liturgy begins with the ministers' silent entrance and prostration before the altar. The celebration has three parts. First, the Liturgy of the Word centers on the proclamation of the Passion according to John, followed by an extended form of the Intercessions. The second part of the celebration is the Veneration of the Cross, giving all due honor to the instrument of our salvation while remembering Jesus' sacrificial love. In the final part of the celebration, Holy Communion is distributed to the faithful. Because Mass may not be celebrated on Good Friday, Communion is distributed from the hosts reserved from the Mass of the Lord's Supper.

Holy Saturday is spent in silence, prayer, and vigil near the tomb of the Lord. After night falls, the Easter Vigil begins. The *Norms* for celebrating the Easter Vigil state:

> The Easter Vigil, in the holy night when the Lord rose again, is considered the "mother of all holy Vigils" (St. Augustine, *Sermo*: 219: PL 38, 1088), in which the Church, keeping watch, awaits the Resurrection of Christ and celebrates it in the Sacraments. Therefore, the entire celebration of this sacred Vigil must take place at night, so that it both begins after nightfall and ends before the dawn on the Sunday. (*Norms*, no. 21)

The liturgy of the vigil begins outside the church with the blessing of the new fire and the preparation of the Paschal Candle. This candle will burn during all Masses throughout the Easter season as well as at Baptisms and funerals throughout the year. The faithful enter the church behind the Paschal Candle hailing Christ, the true light. This first part of the vigil ends with the proclamation of the Exsultet, an ancient hymn of thanksgiving for the candle and a reflection on the gift of salvation.

The second part of the Easter Vigil is an extended Liturgy of the Word. Nine readings are assigned, each with its own Psalm and prayer. The first seven readings, taken from the Old Testament, trace salvation history from the creation of the world to the time of the prophets. The Epistle is taken from St. Paul's Letter to the Romans and reflects on the mystery of Baptism and our incorporation into Christ. After the joyful proclamation of the Easter *Alleluia*, the Gospel recounts the Resurrection. While the number of readings from the Old Testament may be reduced for serious pastoral reasons, at least three, including the crossing of the Red Sea, should be used and their Responsorial Psalms sung.

In the third part of the Easter Vigil, the Sacraments of Baptism and Confirmation are celebrated. In addition to those adults and older children called to the Sacraments of Initiation at the beginning of Lent, parishes may choose to baptize infants and young children. A parish that is not celebrating Baptisms may simply bless the baptismal font and invite all present to renew their baptismal vows. Typically, adults baptized at the Easter Vigil are confirmed at the vigil as well. In addition, the vigil provides an opportunity for many parishes to receive candidates into the full communion of the Church. Such candidates renew their baptismal promises, make a profession of faith, and, usually, are confirmed. Candidates who have been validly confirmed previously (for example, in the Orthodox Church) are not confirmed again.

The Easter Vigil concludes with the celebration of the Eucharist where the newly baptized and received are welcomed to the Eucharistic table for the first time.

Easter Sunday is the final day of the Triduum. In the dioceses of the United States, the faithful are invited to renew their baptismal promises, after which they are sprinkled with the newly blessed water. The Triduum concludes with the solemn celebration of the Vespers of Easter.

O God, who on this day,
through your Only Begotten Son,
have conquered death
and unlocked for us the path to eternity,
grant, we pray, that we who keep
the solemnity of the Lord's Resurrection
may, through the renewal brought by your Spirit,
rise up in the light of life.
Through our Lord Jesus Christ, your Son,
who lives and reigns with you in the unity of the Holy Spirit,
one God, for ever and ever.

(Collect, Easter Sunday of the Resurrection of the Lord,
At the Mass During the Day, *Roman Missal*)

EASTER

aster does not end as the sun sets on Sunday. Rather, Easter Sunday begins the Octave of Easter. Each of these eight days is a solemnity, a continuation of the celebration of Easter. The Gospel readings assigned to these days focus on Jesus' post-Resurrection appearances. The eighth and final day of the Octave, the Second Sunday of Easter, is also called Divine Mercy Sunday. This observance, established by Blessed Pope John Paul II, "concentrates on the mercy poured forth in Christ's death and resurrection, fount of the Holy Spirit who forgives sins and restores joy at having been redeemed" (*Directory*, no. 154).

The celebration of Easter, the greatest feast of the Church, does not end in only eight days. "*Easter* is not simply one feast among others, but the 'Feast of feasts,' the 'Solemnity of solemnities'" (CCC, no. 1169). As such, the celebration of Easter extends for fifty days. "The fifty days from the Sunday of the Resurrection to Pentecost Sunday are celebrated in joy and exultation as one feast day, indeed as one 'great Sunday.' These are the days above all others in which

the *Alleluia* is sung" (*Norms*, no. 22). In these fifty days, the time of mystagogy, the newly baptized and received reflect on the sacraments they have received. The first readings throughout the season of Easter are taken from the Acts of the Apostles, recounting the earliest days of the Church. The Gospel readings are taken from the Gospel of John.

Gladden us with holy joys, almighty God,
and make us rejoice with devout thanksgiving,
for the Ascension of Christ your Son
is our exaltation,
and, where the Head has gone before in glory,
the Body is called to follow in hope.
Through our Lord Jesus Christ, your Son,
who lives and reigns with you in the unity of the Holy Spirit,
one God, for ever and ever.

(Collect, The Ascension of the Lord,
At the Mass During the Day, *Roman Missal*)

The Solemnity of the Ascension of the Lord is celebrated on the fortieth day after Easter (or on the Sunday following as described above). "The mystery of the Ascension has been interpreted to mean that Christ's human nature is taken up into the realm and mystery of the divine Trinity. In the divinization of Christ's *human* nature is the hope for the glorification and divinization of our own humanity" (*Holy Days*, 44). Thus, in the celebration of the Ascension, we catch a glimpse of what we hope someday to be: caught up in the mystery of divine love that is the Trinity.

The days between the Solemnity of the Ascension and the Solemnity of Pentecost are days of intense prayer for the coming of the Holy Spirit. When the Ascension is observed on the Thursday, this time of prayer comprises a novena.

Grant, we pray, almighty God,
that the splendor of your glory
may shine forth upon us
and that, by the bright rays of the Holy Spirit,
the light of your light may confirm the hearts
of those born again by your grace.
Through our Lord Jesus Christ, your Son,
who lives and reigns with you in the unity of the Holy Spirit,
one God, for ever and ever.

(Collect, Pentecost Sunday,
At the Vigil Mass, *Roman Missal*)

The Solemnity of Pentecost, on the fiftieth day of Easter, concludes the Easter Season. In recent years, the Church has restored the extended vigil for this solemnity. Similar to the Easter Vigil, the vigil of Pentecost includes four readings from the Old Testament, each with a proper Psalm and prayer, along with the Epistle and Gospel. At the conclusion of the Mass during the Day, the Paschal Candle is extinguished and moved to its permanent location near the baptismal font.

ORDINARY TIME

he remaining weeks of the year belong to Ordinary Time. The title Ordinary Time does not imply that these weeks lack importance. The name "Ordinary" is used because their names are derived from the ordinal numbers, thus, the Third Week in Ordinary Time, the Eleventh Week in Ordinary Time, and so on. In these weeks, "no particular aspect of the mystery of Christ is celebrated, but rather the mystery of Christ itself is honored in its fullness, especially on Sundays" (*Norms*, no. 43). These weeks allow us to reflect carefully on Jesus' ministry—his preaching, his parables, and his miracles.

The Sunday after Pentecost is the Solemnity of the Most Holy Trinity. "With the growth of devotion to the mystery of God in His Unity and Trinity, John XXII extended the feast of the Holy Trinity to the entire Latin Church in 1334" (*Directory*, no. 157). The Sunday following Trinity Sunday is celebrated as the Solemnity of the Body and Blood of Christ (in much of the Church, this feast is celebrated on the preceding Thursday). "This feast is both a doctrinal and cultic response to heretical teaching on the mystery of the real presence of Christ in the Eucharist, and the apogee of an ardent devotional movement concentrated on the Sacrament of the Altar. It was extended to the entire Latin Church by Urban

IV in 1264" (*Directory*, no. 160). In many places, this solemnity is celebrated with public processions of the Blessed Sacrament and extended periods of Eucharistic adoration. These Sundays replace the Sundays in Ordinary Time, though the weeks following are numbered. Similarly, the week after the Feast of the Baptism of the Lord is the First Week in Ordinary Time.

LAST DAYS OF ORDINARY TIME

he final weeks of Ordinary Time turn our focus to the end times, when the world as we know it will end, Christ will come as judge, and God's kingdom with be established, "on earth as it is in heaven." Thus, it is most appropriate that the final Sunday of Ordinary Time (and of the liturgical year) is celebrated as the Solemnity of Christ, King of the Universe. In these weeks, we are called to prepare ourselves for the day when Christ will come "to judge the living and the dead . . . [and] reveal the secret disposition of hearts" (CCC, no. 682).

III. THE PROPER
OF SAINTS

Alongside the Proper of Time, the liturgical calendar includes the Proper of Saints. The Proper of Saints allows us to recall those who have gone before us in faith, learning from and inspired by their heroic witness. First among the saints is the Blessed Virgin Mary, and, accordingly, many feasts of the Blessed Virgin are part of the liturgical calendar. The *Catechism* expounds on the purposeful commemoration of the Blessed Virgin and other Saints throughout the year:

> When the Church keeps the memorials of martyrs and other saints during the annual cycle, she proclaims the Paschal mystery in those "who have suffered and have been glorified with Christ. She proposes them to the faithful as examples who draw all men to the Father through Christ, and through their merits she begs for God's favors." (CCC no. 1173, quoting the *Constitution on the Sacred Liturgy*, no. 104; see nos. 108, 111)

With the revision of the liturgical calendar after the Second Vatican Council, the number of saints' days listed on the General Roman Calendar (observed throughout the Church) has decreased so that "the feasts of the Saints may not take precedence over commemorations of the mysteries of salvation" (*Directory*, no. 228, quoting *Constitution on the Sacred Liturgy*, no. 111). The *Directory* goes on to emphasize that

> it is necessary to instruct the faithful on the links between the feasts of the Saints and the commemoration of the mystery of salvation of Christ. The *raison d'etre* for the feasts of the Saints is to highlight concrete realizations of the saving plan of God and "to proclaim the marvels of Christ in his servants" (*Constitution on the Sacred Liturgy*, no. 111); the feasts accorded to the Saints, the members of the Body of Christ, are ultimately feasts of the Head who is Christ. (*Directory*, no. 229)

JANUARY

**1   *The Octave Day of the Nativity of the Lord*:
*Solemnity of Mary, the Holy Mother of God***

Please see the discussion of the Christmas
season above.

**2   *SS. Basil the Great and Gregory Nazianzen,
Bishops and Doctors of the Church, Memorial***

Basil and Gregory were friends born in the eastern regions of the Mediterranean in Asia Minor.
Though both spent time as hermits, they answered
the call to serve the Church as bishops. Their
theological writings, including Basil's monastic
Rule, continue to inform the Church's faith.

3   *The Most Holy Name of Jesus*[3]

Scripture affirms that Jesus is the only name by
which we are to be saved and the name that we
must honor above all.

---

3   When the rank of the celebration is not indicated, it is an optional memorial.

4   [USA] St. Elizabeth Ann Seton, Religious, Memorial

Elizabeth Ann Seton was received into the Catholic Church as an adult because of the lived witness of faith of her Catholic friends. The first saint born in the United States, she is noted for founding the Daughters of Charity and building the foundation of the Catholic school system.

5   [USA] St. John Neumann, Bishop, Memorial

Born in Bohemia, John Neumann travelled to the United States as a young adult. There, he was ordained a priest and began his work with immigrants. After joining the Redemptorist Order, he became the bishop of Philadelphia, where he was noted for his continued work with immigrants and for expanding the parishes and schools in the diocese.

6   [USA] St. André Bessette, Religious

Born in Canada, André Bessette was a member of the Congregation of the Holy Cross. Within the order, his primary task was to serve as porter, opening the door and welcoming visitors. His devotion to God and to St. Joseph inspired his religious brothers and all who came in contact with him.

7   *St. Raymond of Penyafort, Priest*

A worldwide leader of the Dominican Order, Raymond was noted for his skill in administration, his knowledge of canon law, and his extensive writing on the celebration of the Sacrament of Penance.

13   *St. Hilary, Bishop and Doctor of the Church*

Hilary served as bishop of Poitiers, where he was acclaimed for his theological works that upheld orthodoxy of faith. Many of his works focus on the proper interpretation of Scripture.

17   *St. Anthony, Abbot, Memorial*

Anthony is considered the father of monasticism. He chose voluntary poverty and seclusion so as to focus his life solely on the Lord. As other men gathered around him to share this life, he led them in faithful devotion.

20 St. Fabian, Pope and Martyr

A third-century Bishop of Rome, Fabian was martyred in the Decian persecution.

St. Sebastian, Martyr

Sebastian was martyred during the Diocletian persecution. He is recalled in numerous artistic depictions undergoing the torture of being pierced by many arrows. Surprisingly, this torture did not lead to his death. Rather, he was martyred by clubbing.

21 St. Agnes, Virgin and Martyr, Memorial

Agnes was martyred in the early centuries of the Church's history, though the exact date is unknown. Because her name is derived from the Latin word for lamb (*agnus*), on this date, the pope blesses the lambs whose wool will be used to weave the pallia (a special vestment worn over the shoulders by archbishops).

22 [USA] Day of Prayer for the Legal Protection of Unborn Children[4]

On January 22, 1973, the U.S. Supreme Court issued the *Roe v. Wade* and *Doe v. Bolton* rulings, abrogating state laws restricting abortion. In the dioceses of the United States, this day is observed as a day of special prayer for the legal protection of unborn children and of greatest reverence for the sanctity of human life as a gift of God.

23 [USA] St. Vincent, Deacon and Martyr

Vincent, a deacon in the Church in Spain, was martyred during the Diocletian persecution.

24 St. Francis de Sales, Bishop and Doctor of the Church, Memorial

The bishop of Geneva, Francis de Sales was noted for his skill as a pastor. His masterwork, *Introduction to the Devout Life*, remains a standard for spiritual directors and for all seeking to grow in the spiritual life.

---

4   January 23, when January 22 falls on a Sunday.

25 *The Conversion of St. Paul the Apostle, Feast*
In his first appearance in the Acts of the Apostles, Paul, then called Saul, stands watch at the martyrdom of Stephen. On a trip to Damascus—to arrest more Christians—Paul encountered the Risen Jesus and became one of the greatest preachers of the Gospel the world has ever known.

26 *SS. Timothy and Titus, Bishops, Memorial*

Timothy and Titus assisted Paul in his missionary efforts and ultimately served as bishops of Ephesus and Crete, respectively. The New Testament letters to Timothy and Titus were addressed to them, providing excellent advice about living a life of faith and leading Christ's Church.

27 *St. Angela Merici, Virgin*

Angela Merici founded the Ursuline Order, dedicated to providing education to girls, especially poor girls.

28 St. Thomas Aquinas, Priest and Doctor of the Church, Memorial

One of the greatest theologians in Church history, Thomas Aquinas' thought shaped thinking in the Church for almost a millennium. His personal spiritual devotion was as great as his intellect.

31 St. John Bosco, Priest, Memorial

John Bosco is best known for his efforts to educate youth and to help them develop their faith. These efforts include both the publication of educational materials and training in practical arts.

Sunday between January 2 and January 8: [USA] The Epiphany of the Lord, Solemnity

Sunday after January 6: The Baptism of the Lord, Feast

For these observances, see the discussion under "Christmas."

FEBRUARY

2   *The Presentation of the Lord, Feast*

This feast, forty days after Christmas, celebrates the Presentation of Jesus in the Jerusalem Temple, in accordance with the law of the Lord. Simeon and Anna, who had been waiting with faith and hope, saw Jesus in the Temple and recognized him as the Messiah. Also known as Candlemas, on this day the Church blesses the candles it will use in the coming year, a recognition that Christ is light to the nations.

3   *St. Blaise, Bishop and Martyr*

This Armenian bishop was martyred in the fourth century. Because he is the patron saint of those with throat ailments, on this day, it is traditional to bless the throats of the faithful using candles blessed on the previous day.

St. Ansgar, Bishop

Though born and raised in France, Ansgar is noted for his lifelong efforts to preach the Gospel in Scandinavia, particularly what is now Denmark and Sweden.

5 St. Agatha, Virgin and Martyr, Memorial

Martyred during the Decian persecution, honor for Agatha spread throughout the early Church. Her name is included in the Roman Canon (Eucharistic Prayer I).

6 St. Paul Miki and Companions, Martyrs, Memorial

A member of the Society of Jesus (the Jesuits), Paul Miki preached the Gospel in Japan. He was martyred by crucifixion along with twenty-five companions.

8 St. Jerome Emiliani

Abandoning a military career, Jerome Emiliani embraced poverty and spent his remaining life assisting the poor, especially orphans.

St. Josephine Bakhita, Virgin

Born in Sudan, she came to Italy as a slave. While in Italy, she converted to Catholicism, eventually becoming a nun. She was noted for her forgiveness and her abiding hope through life's struggles.

10 *St. Scholastica, Virgin, Memorial*

Scholastica was the sister of St. Benedict. She founded an order of religious women near her brother's monastery for men. The two met regularly to discuss religious life and spiritual matters.

11 *Our Lady of Lourdes*

In 1858, the Blessed Virgin appeared to Bernadette Soubirous near Lourdes, France. The Blessed Virgin called the people to prayer and penance and to care for the poor and ill. Today, Lourdes remains a place of pilgrimage for those who are ill. The World Day of Prayer for the Sick is celebrated on this day.

14 *SS. Cyril, Monk, and Methodius, Bishop, Memorial*

Cyril and Methodius were brothers who traveled to the Slavic countries of Eastern Europe to preach the Gospel. They are credited with preparing liturgical books in the language of the people, using an alphabet that bears Cyril's name.

17   The Seven Holy Founders of the Servite Order

These seven young men of wealthy families in Florence founded a religious order devoted to the Blessed Virgin. The Servites are one of the five original mendicant orders of the Church.

21   St. Peter Damian, Bishop and Doctor of the Church

This eleventh-century bishop and cardinal worked to promote and renew religious life and the Church in general.

22   The Chair of St. Peter the Apostle, Feast

This feast celebrates the unity of the Church founded upon Peter, its Rock.

23   St. Polycarp, Bishop and Martyr, Memorial

Polycarp was bishop of Smyrna in the second century. Reputed to be a disciple of the Apostle John, he in turn taught St. Ignatius of Antioch. He was martyred in the amphitheater of his home city.

MARCH

3 *[USA] St. Katharine Drexel, Virgin*

Born into a wealthy Philadelphia family, Katharine Drexel used her fortune to provide for the needs and education of African Americans and Native Americans, establishing many schools, including Xavier University in New Orleans. She founded a religious order of women to carry on this work.

4 *St. Casimir*

The son of the King of Poland, Casimir lived his life with great religious devotion, particularly to the Blessed Virgin, and to care for the poor.

7 *SS. Perpetua and Felicity, Martyrs, Memorial*

Martyred in Carthage, these young mothers were noted for their great bravery in facing martyrdom and in their assurance that they would share in Christ's Resurrection.

8 *St. John of God, Religious*

St. John of God devoted himself to the care of the sick, particularly those who were poor. He founded a religious order of men who carry on this work today.

9 St. Frances of Rome, Religious

Though a wealthy young matron, Frances gave much of her wealth to the poor. After her sons died prematurely, she founded a religious order despite her many illnesses.

17 St. Patrick, Bishop

Born in Britain, Patrick was taken to Ireland as a slave. After his release, he returned to Ireland to preach the Gospel. He is often called "the Apostle to Ireland."

18 St. Cyril of Jerusalem, Bishop and Doctor of the Church

This fourth-century bishop of Jerusalem is best known for his catechetical sermons, which reflect on faith and the sacraments.

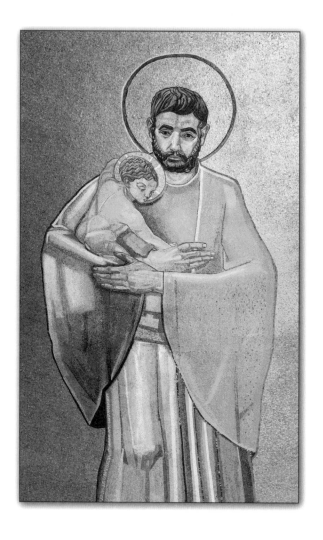

19 St. Joseph, Spouse of the Blessed Virgin Mary, Solemnity

Joseph was the husband of Mary and the foster father of Jesus. He raised Jesus as his own son, giving him protection and care.

> The virtues of St. Joseph have been the object of ecclesial reflection down through the centuries, especially the more recent centuries. Among those virtues the following stand out: faith, with which he fully accepted God's salvific plan; prompt and silent obedience to the will of God; love for and fulfillment of the law, true piety, fortitude in time of trial; chaste love for the Blessed Virgin Mary, a dutiful exercise of his paternal authority, and fruitful reticence. (*Directory*, no. 219)

When this solemnity falls on a Sunday in Lent, it is transferred to the Monday. On this solemnity, even in Lent, we sing the *Gloria*. If it falls on a Friday in Lent, the obligation to abstain from meat is lifted.

23 *St. Turibius of Mogrovejo, Bishop*

Born in Spain, Turibius traveled to the "New World" to become bishop of Lima. He worked diligently to spread the faith throughout Latin America and to care for the native population.

25 *The Annunciation of the Lord, Solemnity*

This solemnity recalls the Archangel Gabriel's visit to Mary to announce that God had chosen her to become the Mother of his Son. Nine months before the Nativity of the Lord, it celebrates the Incarnation of Christ in the womb of the Blessed Virgin. When this solemnity falls on a Sunday in Lent, it is transferred to the nearest Monday. On this solemnity, even in Lent, we sing the *Gloria*. If it falls on a Friday in Lent, the obligation to abstain from meat is lifted.

APRIL

2 *St. Francis of Paola, Hermit*

Though he began his life as a Franciscan friar, he founded an order of hermits who lived in seclusion and led lives of great humility and deprivation.

4 *St. Isidore, Bishop and Doctor of the Church*

Serving as Bishop of Seville in Spain, Isidore led many Church councils with great wisdom. He promoted the preservation of knowledge and compiled an encyclopedia of general knowledge. Because of his attempts to organize available knowledge, some consider him the patron saint of the Internet.

5 *St. Vincent Ferrer, Priest*

Vincent Ferrer was a Dominican priest best known for the excellence of his preaching on the avoidance of sin and living a virtuous life so that, in the final judgment, one might be admitted to heaven.

7   *St. John Baptist de la Salle, Priest, Memorial*

A priest in France, John the Baptist de la Salle focused his ministry on the education of boys. He founded many schools for the poor.

11   *St. Stanislaus, Bishop and Martyr, Memorial*

The bishop of Krakow, Poland, Stanislaus was martyred by the king. He has been venerated in Poland since his death.

13   *St. Martin I, Pope and Martyr*

This seventh-century pope promoted authentic teaching about the nature and will of Christ. Abducted and imprisoned by the emperor, he died of his privations.

21   *St. Anselm, Bishop and Doctor of the Church*

One of the great thinkers of the Church, Anselm's writings continue to influence theology today. He served as the archbishop of Canterbury.

23 St. George, Martyr

Born to Christian parents, George served as a Roman soldier in Palestine. He was martyred for refusing to renounce his Christianity and offer sacrifice to the emperor. He is the patron saint of soldiers and England.

St. Adalbert, Bishop and Martyr

This bishop of Prague was noted for his efforts at evangelization and his encouragement to the baptized to live authentically Christian lives. He was martyred while serving as a missionary to Prussia.

24 St. Fidelis of Sigmaringen, Priest and Martyr

A Capuchin friar, Fidelis lived a life of great austerity and dedicated himself to preaching. He was martyred by Calvinist soldiers in Switzerland.

25 St. Mark, Evangelist, Feast

Mark accompanied St. Paul on his first missionary journey and on his trip to Rome. The second of the four Gospels bears Mark's name. Mark is considered the founder of the Church in Alexandria and is the patron saint of Venice.

28   St. Peter Chanel, Priest and Martyr

This Marist missionary traveled to the South Pacific to spread the Good News of Jesus Christ. Through his martyrdom, he inspired the conversion of many.

St. Louis Grignion de Montfort, Priest

This French priest is noted for his influential teaching on the importance of dedication to God alone and to his understanding that people can come to Christ through his Mother Mary.

29   St. Catherine of Siena, Virgin and Doctor of the Church, Memorial

Catherine worked to end the Avignon Papacy and return the pope to the city of Rome. Her great spiritual works focus on mystical marriage to Christ and divine providence. Her correspondence with religious and others reflects on the religious questions of her day.

30   St. Pius V, Pope

Pope Pius V enforced the decrees of the Council of Trent. Among his best-known efforts are the promulgation of the 1570 *Roman Missal*, used for almost four hundred years, and his efforts to protect Europe from the Ottoman Empire.

MAY

1   St. Joseph the Worker

In many parts of the world, May 1 is celebrated as Labor Day. On this day, the Church celebrates St. Joseph as a model for all workers, noting that his work as a carpenter supported the Holy Family. This observance speaks to the dignity of human work as participation in God's work of creation.

2   St. Athanasius, Bishop and Doctor of the Church, Memorial

This bishop of Alexandria is best known for his ardent defense of the true faith and his numerous writings, particularly his denial of the Arian heresy, which denied Jesus' consubstantiality with the Father.

3   SS. Philip and James, Apostles, Feast

At first Philip followed John the Baptist, but later he came to Jesus. James was the son of Alphaeus, not Zebedee. Both were counted among the Twelve Apostles who traveled with Jesus throughout his ministry.

10 *[USA] St. Damien de Veuster, Priest*

Born in Belgium, Damien traveled to Hawaii, where he was ordained to the priesthood. He spent his life ministering to those suffering from leprosy in the leper colony on Molakai. Eventually, he succumbed to the disease himself.

12 *SS. Nereus and Achilleus, Martyrs*

These men began their careers as soldiers in the Roman army. Upon leaving the army after their conversion to Christianity, they suffered martyrdom.

St. Pancras, Martyr

Though little is known of his life, Pancras is reputed to have been martyred at the age of fourteen, remaining strong in his faith despite his youth.

13 *Our Lady of Fatima*

This feast commemorates the appearances of the Blessed Virgin Mary in Fatima, Portugal, in 1917. She appeared six times to three poor children, speaking of the necessity of penance and reparation for sin.

14   St. Matthias, Apostle, Feast

The first chapter of the Acts of the Apostles recounts Matthias's selection to take the place of Judas among the Twelve Apostles. Matthias had traveled with Jesus during his ministry and was a witness to the Resurrection.

15   [USA] St. Isidore

Isidore the Farmer was a peasant and day laborer in Spain. He and his wife, Maria, also a canonized saint, were widely known and honored for their great religious devotion.

18   St. John I, Pope and Martyr

This sixth-century pope traveled to Constantinople as an ambassador to the Roman Emperor. He was imprisoned by the king upon his return from Constantinople and died from neglect in prison.

20   St. Bernardine of Siena, Priest

Bernardine was widely known as a great preacher and for his devotion to the Holy Name of Jesus.

21 St. Christopher Magallanes, Priest, and Companions, Martyrs

Christopher Magallenes served as a parish priest in Mexico, noted for his spiritual direction of seminarians and his promotion of the holy Rosary. He and his companions were martyred amid the anti-clerical sentiment of the early twentieth century.

22 St. Rita of Cascia, Religious

Married at a young age to an abusive husband, Rita dissuaded her sons from taking revenge when her husband was murdered. Entering the convent after becoming a widow, she was known for her forgiving spirit and great devotion to the Lord.

25 St. Bede the Venerable, Priest and Doctor of the Church

Called venerable, even though he is a saint, Bede is well known for his scholarly works on history, astronomy, education, and poetry, and for his writing on Sacred Scripture.

St. Gregory VII, Pope

Best known for his dispute with the Holy Roman Emperor Henry IV over the role of secular authorities in the appointment of Church leaders, Gregory also worked on behalf of reform in the Church and to promote belief in the Real Presence of Jesus Christ in the Sacrament of the Eucharist.

St. Mary Magdalene de' Pazzi, Virgin

A Carmelite nun, Mary Magdalene de' Pazzi lived a life of great devotion and humility, far from the wealth and status into which she was born. Her mystical writings include brilliant reflections on the Holy Spirit.

26　St. Philip Neri, Priest, Memorial

Philip Neri founded an order of priests dedicated to care for the poor, especially pilgrims, and for the sick who were released from hospitals, but not yet able to return to work. The order is noted for its devotion to spiritual reading and music.

27 *St. Augustine of Canterbury, Bishop*

Augustine was the first archbishop of Canterbury and is regarded as the founder of the English Church for his role in preaching the Gospel in Britain and converting many.

31 *The Visitation of the Blessed Virgin Mary, Feast*

This feast commemorates the trip recounted in the first chapter of Luke's Gospel regarding Mary's journey to visit her elderly kinswoman, Elizabeth, then pregnant with John the Baptist. Elizabeth greets Mary with a profession of faith, and Mary responds with the beautiful words of the Magnificat (see Lk 1:46-55).

First Sunday after Pentecost: The Most Holy Trinity, Solemnity

Sunday after the Most Holy Trinity: [USA] The Most Holy Body and Blood of Christ, Solemnity

For these observances, see the discussion under "Ordinary Time" (pp. 37-38).

JUNE

1 St. Justin, Martyr, Memorial

Though born to pagan parents, Justin converted to Christianity and became an ardent defender of the faith. He used his training in philosophy to dispute those who disagreed with the faith and to defend his beliefs.

2 SS. Marcellinus and Peter, Martyrs

Little is known about these martyrs. Pope Damasus I reported that these men were martyred during the Diocletian persecution. They were beheaded in a grove outside the city so that other Christians could not venerate their tomb, but their bodies were discovered and a basilica built over their tombs.

3 St. Charles Lwanga and Companions, Martyrs, Memorial

Charles Lwanga and his companions were young men serving in the court of King Mwanga of Uganda. Charles served as a catechist, helping to form the faith of his companions. The king had them executed for refusing to renounce their Christianity.

5   *St. Boniface, Bishop and Martyr, Memorial*

In the eighth century, Boniface traveled from England to preach the Gospel in Germany, and he served as the first bishop of Mainz. He is known as a great missionary who did much to bring order to the Church and clergy in his region and to unify Europe.

6   *St. Norbert, Bishop*

After a grave accident, Norbert reformed his life and became a well-known preacher throughout France and Germany. He founded the Premonstratensian (Norbertine) Order and worked tirelessly to reform clerical life and to spread the faith.

9   *St. Ephrem, Deacon and Doctor of the Church*

Born in Syria, Ephrem served the Church there throughout his life. He is known for his brilliant theological writings, including hymns, explanations of Scripture, and refutations of theological errors.

11   *St. Barnabas, Apostle, Memorial*

Barnabas was one of the earliest followers of Christ, though not one of the Twelve. He accompanied Paul on his first missionary journey and preached the Gospel in Antioch.

13 *St. Anthony of Padua, Priest and Doctor of the Church, Memorial*

Though best known as the patron of those seeking lost objects, in his own time, Anthony was regarded as a brilliant preacher, noted for both his wisdom and his kindness. He was the first Franciscan charged with teaching theology to members of the order.

19 *St. Romuald, Abbot*

Romuald lived much of his life as a hermit, though he founded many monasteries and the Camaldolese Monks. He called all monks to the qualities of life for which he was known: self-denial, solitude, and devotion to the Psalms.

21 *St. Aloysius Gonzaga, Religious, Memorial*

Aloysius Gonazaga renounced his wealth and privilege to join the Society of Jesus, hoping to become a missionary. Unable to become a missionary due to his poor health, he died at the age of twenty-three while serving in a hospital for plague victims. He was known for his devotion to the Blessed Virgin Mary and for his purity.

22 St. Paulinus of Nola, Bishop

Paulinus was a Roman senator who converted to Christianity and received Baptism after marrying a Christian woman. After the death of their son, Paulinus and his wife withdrew to religious life. After his wife's death, Paulinus became bishop of Nola. He is known for promoting the veneration of St. Felix of Nola and for his exceptional Latin poetry.

SS. John Fisher, Bishop, and Thomas More, Martyrs

John Fisher served as bishop of Rochester and Thomas More as chancellor of England in the difficult days of the Reformation and the breach between Henry VIII and the Church. Both strongly defended the faith against the theological errors of the time. Both were executed for their opposition to the king's divorce from Catherine of Aragon.

24 The Nativity of St. John the Baptist, Solemnity

This solemnity commemorates the birth of John the Baptist, who would become Jesus' herald. John's nativity is celebrated near the summer solstice, as Jesus' Nativity is celebrated at the winter solstice. The Mass has a proper vigil, and the solemnity replaces the Mass of the day when it occurs on a Sunday in Ordinary Time.

27 St. Cyril of Alexandria, Bishop and Doctor of the Church

Cyril served as Bishop of Alexandria in the fifth century when that city was a center of power and learning. He is best known for his defense of the belief that Mary is the *Theotokos*, the Mother of God, a title confirmed by the Council of Ephesus, which Cyril attended.

28 St. Irenaeus, Bishop and Martyr, Memorial

A student of St. Polycarp in Smyrna, Irenaeus served as a priest and bishop in Lyons. His theological writings defended the faith from the Gnostic heresies. He was martyred with other Christians at the beginning of the third century.

29 SS. Peter and Paul, Apostles, Solemnity

These two great saints are celebrated jointly, recognizing their pivotal roles in the foundation and growth of the early Church. The Rock on which the Church was founded and the Apostle to the Gentiles both suffered martyrdom in the city of Rome, likely during the persecution of Nero. The Mass has a proper vigil, and the solemnity replaces the Mass of the day when it occurs on a Sunday in Ordinary Time.

30 *The First Martyrs of the Holy Roman Church*

This observance recalls the faithful men and women martyred by Nero in the city of Rome in 64 during the first widespread persecution of Christians.

Friday after the Second Sunday after Pentecost: The Most Sacred Heart of Jesus, Solemnity

On this great solemnity, we honor the Sacred Heart of Jesus, overflowing with love, mercy, and compassion for all who would call on him. "The Solemnity of the Sacred Heart celebrates the salvific mysteries of Christ in a synthetic manner by reducing them to their fount—the Heart of Jesus" (*Directory*, no. 174). In recent years, this solemnity has become a special day of prayer for the sanctity of priests.

Saturday after the Second Sunday after Pentecost: The Immaculate Heart of the Blessed Virgin Mary, Memorial

The Church celebrates the liturgical memorial of the Immaculate Heart of Mary the day after the Solemnity of the Sacred Heart of Jesus. The contiguity of both celebrations is in itself a liturgical sign of their close connection: the *mysterium* of the Heart of Jesus is projected onto and reverberates in the Heart of His Mother, who is also one of his followers and a disciple. . . . Following the apparitions at Fatima in 1917, devotion to the Immaculate Heart of Mary became very widespread. On the twenty-fifth anniversary of the apparitions (1942) Pius XII consecrated the Church and the human race to the Immaculate Heart of Mary, and extended the memorial to the entire Church. (*Directory*, no. 174)

JULY

1   [USA] *Blessed Junípero Serra, Priest*

Junípero Serra was a Franciscan priest sent as a missionary to Mexico in 1749. He later traveled to California where he established nine missions to serve as centers of evangelization and worship.

3   *St. Thomas, Apostle, Feast*

Best known as "Doubting Thomas" for his lack of belief in the other Apostles' report that they had seen the Risen Jesus, Thomas expressed his faith when he encountered the Lord the following week. Tradition holds that he carried the faith to India, where he suffered a martyr's death.

4   [USA] *Independence Day*

On this anniversary of the Declaration of Independence, the dioceses of the United States may use proper orations and a proper Preface to pray that the nation will remain a place of "liberty and justice for all."

5 *St. Anthony Zaccaria, Priest*

After training and working as a doctor, Anthony Mary Zaccaria was ordained a priest. He founded three religious orders: one for men, one for women, and one for married couples. He promoted devotion to the Crucifixion of Christ and reverence for the Eucharist, beginning the Forty Hours Devotion as a period of Eucharistic exposition and adoration.

[USA] St. Elizabeth of Portugal

Serving as Queen of Portugal, Elizabeth was known for her steadfast faith in affliction and her charity toward the poor. She served as a peacemaker between her husband and son and later between her son and son-in-law. In her widowhood, she retired to a monastery and continued her acts of charity.

6 *St. Maria Goretti, Virgin and Martyr*

Noted for piety even as a child, Maria Goretti was stabbed to death rather than be raped. She forgave her murderer before she died.

9 St. Augustine Zhao Rong, Priest, and Companions, Martyrs

Augustine Zhao Rong was a soldier who converted to Christianity because of the example of a missionary priest. After being baptized and studying the faith, he was ordained a priest and served in a Chinese diocese. He was martyred in 1815. On this day, we recall all the missionaries and faithful in China who were martyred for their faith.

11 St. Benedict, Abbot, Memorial

Called the "Father of Western Monasticism," Benedict established a monastery for men at Monte Cassino and wrote the Rule that has guided monastic life ever since.

13 St. Henry

This Holy Roman Emperor gave great attention to Church reform and promoted missionary activity.

14 [USA] St. Kateri Tekakwitha, Virgin, Memorial

The daughter of Mohawk and Algonquin parents, Kateri was left an orphan by a smallpox epidemic that disfigured her. Converting to Christianity, she lived a life of penance and purity.

15 St. Bonaventure, Bishop and Doctor of the Church, Memorial

A Franciscan and eventually leader of the order, Bonaventure is one of the great theologians of the Middle Ages, writing with great insight on faith and philosophy.

16 Our Lady of Mount Carmel

Mount Carmel is traditionally recognized as the mountain on which the prophet Elijah defeated the prophets of Baal. It is home to an order of priests who live a contemplative life, with emphasis on devotion to Mary.

18 [USA] St. Camillus de Lellis, Priest

A former soldier, Camillus de Lellis founded a religious order to care for the sick, initially focusing on the wounded soldiers left on the battlefield. The symbol of this order was a red cross on a white cassock.

20 St. Apollinaris, Bishop and Martyr

A native of Antioch, Apollinaris served as bishop of Ravenna before being martyred, likely in the late second century.

21   *St. Lawrence of Brindisi, Priest and Doctor of the Church*

A Capuchin friar, Lawrence led his order and served the Holy See in a variety of capacities. His knowledge of languages and his skill in preaching helped him to encourage many people to return to the practice of the faith.

22   *St. Mary Magdalene, Memorial*

One of Christ's most faithful disciples, Mary Magdalene was present at the Crucifixion and was the first witness to the Resurrection, carrying the Good News to the Apostles. In the East, she is known as "the apostle to the Apostles."

23   *St. Bridget, Religious*

Bridget was a devoted wife and mother in Sweden. After her husband's death, she first undertook a life of asceticism and penance before founding a religious order. She was noted for her virtue and her mystical experiences.

24 St. Sharbel Makhluf, Priest

Sharbel was a Maronite monk who spent much of his life living as a hermit in complete silence.

25 St. James, Apostle, Feast

One of the sons of Zebedee, he joined Peter and John as a witness to many of Jesus' miracles, including the Transfiguration and the raising of Jairus's daughter. He was martyred by Herod, making him the first Apostle to suffer this fate.

26 SS. Joachim and Anne, Parents of the Blessed Virgin Mary, Memorial

Tradition gives the names of the Blessed Virgin Mary's parents as Joachim and Anne. They are venerated for their daughter's great virtue and her selection to be the mother of God's Son.

29 St. Martha, Memorial

The sister of Mary and Lazarus. She cared for Jesus and his disciples when they visited her home. When her brother Lazarus died, she expressed her faith that Jesus could raise him from the dead.

30 St. Peter Chrysologus, Bishop and Doctor of the Church

Since his nickname means "golden-worded," it is not surprising that this bishop of Ravenna was widely known for his brief but inspiring homilies.

31 St. Ignatius of Loyola, Priest, Memorial

After years as a courtier and soldier, Ignatius underwent a personal conversion and dedicated himself to the religious life. He founded the Society of Jesus (the Jesuits) to serve the pope. His works on spirituality continue to assist the faithful in developing their spiritual lives.

AUGUST

1 *St. Alphonsus Mary Liguori, Bishop and Doctor of the Church, Memorial*

Both a civil and a canon lawyer, Alphonsus Mary Liguori founded the Redemptorist Order. He is noted for his excellent writings on prayer and moral theology.

2 *St. Eusebius of Vercelli, Bishop*

As bishop, Eusebius established monastic life in his diocese and worked to defend the faith from those who denied its truths.

St. Peter Julian Eymard, Priest

A French priest and founder of two religious orders, Peter Julian Eymard was especially devoted to the Blessed Virgin Mary and to the Eucharist. Much of his ministry focused on preparing children for their First Communion and inviting people to return to the reception of Holy Communion.

4 *St. John Mary Vianney, Priest, Memorial*

Known as the Curé of Ars, John Mary Vianney is the patron saint of parish priests. Even during his life, he was widely acclaimed for his good counsel in hearing confessions and for his excellent preaching.

5 *The Dedication of the Basilica of St. Mary Major*

This observance celebrates the anniversary of the Basilica of St. Mary Major in Rome. Pope Sixtus established this basilica after the Council of Ephesus. It is the oldest church dedicated to the Blessed Virgin Mary in the Western Hemisphere.

6 *The Transfiguration of the Lord, Feast*

This feast recalls the occasion on which Jesus appeared before Peter, James, and John, transformed into his glorified form and conversing with Moses and Elijah, representatives of the Law and the Prophets. This feast replaces the Mass of the day when it falls on Sunday.

7   *St. Sixtus II, Pope, and Companions, Martyrs*

Sixtus was arrested while saying Mass in a cemetery. Martyred along with several deacons by Emperor Valerian I, his name is included in the Roman Canon (Eucharistic Prayer I).

St. Cajetan, Priest

Trained as a lawyer, Cajetan co-founded the Congregation of Clerks Regular to combine the spirit of monastic living with more active service to the Church.

8   *St. Dominic, Priest, Memorial*

Founder of the Order of Preachers (the Dominicans), Dominic worked tirelessly to spread devotion to the Rosary and sound theological preaching to combat heresy.

9   *St. Teresa Benedicta of the Cross, Virgin and Martyr*

Born Edith Stein to a Jewish family, she completed her studies in philosophy. She converted to Catholicism after reading the works of St. Teresa of Avila and became a Discalced Carmelite. Since Sr. Teresa Benedicta was a Jewish convert, she was transported to Auschwitz, where she died in 1942.

10 St. Lawrence, Deacon and Martyr, Feast

Known for his great humor and his even greater love for the poor, Lawrence was martyred in the third century.

11 St. Clare, Virgin, Memorial

Born in Assisi, Clare followed the example of St. Francis and founded an order of nuns dedicated to lives of poverty and charity.

12 St. Jane Frances de Chantal, Religious

Jane Frances de Chantal was a Christian wife and mother of six children. After her husband's death, she devoted herself to caring for the poor, founding the Visitation Order with St. Francis de Sales.

13 SS. Pontian, Pope, and Hippolytus, Priest, Martyrs

These Church leaders were sent into exile by Emperor Maximus. They died due to harsh treatment in the mines of Sardinia.

14 St. Maximilian Mary Kolbe, Priest and Martyr, Memorial

A Polish priest devoted to the defense of the faith and to the Immaculate Heart of Mary, he died in the Auschwitz death camp, voluntarily accepting a death sentence to spare a husband and father.

15 The Assumption of the Blessed Virgin Mary, Solemnity

The first name of this solemnity was the Feast of Mary, Mother of God. Later, its name in the East carried over, the Dormition (or Falling Asleep) of Mary. In the West, it became known as the Assumption of the Blessed Virgin Mary (see *Holy Days*, 54).

This solemnity celebrates the fact that Mary's Assumption is "a pledge of the future participation of the members of the mystical Body of Christ in the paschal glory of the Risen Christ." It shows that the Lord "reserves a munificent reward for his humble Servant because of her faithful cooperation with the divine plan, which is a destiny of fullness, happiness, glorification of her immaculate soul, her virginal body, perfect configuration to her Risen Son" (*Directory*, no. 180). The Mass has a proper vigil, and the solemnity replaces the Mass of the day when it occurs on a Sunday in Ordinary Time.

16   St. Stephen of Hungary

As king of Hungary, Stephen was noted for both his great devotion to the faith of the Church and his justice and compassion in ruling his people.

19   St. John Eudes, Priest

A tireless preacher of parish missions, John Eudes founded a religious order to promote seminary formation and another order of women to save women from lives on the street. He was an early promoter of devotion to the Sacred Heart of Jesus and the Immaculate Heart of Mary.

20   St. Bernard, Abbot and Doctor of the Church, Memorial

Bernard served as abbot of the Cistercian monastery at Clairvaux and sought to reform the practice of monasticism, which had grown lax in many places. He helped the Church resolve schisms and wrote treatises on theology and spirituality that continue to inform the faithful.

21   St. Pius X, Pope, Memorial

Pope Pius X served the Church as pope at the beginning of the twentieth century. He strove to renew the Church by encouraging faithful living of Christian virtues and by combatting errors.

22   The Queenship of the Blessed Virgin Mary, Memorial

One week after the celebration of the Assumption, we commemorate the Coronation of Mary as the Queen of Heaven.

23   St. Rose of Lima, Virgin

Born in Lima, Peru, Rose was known for her purity of life and great religious devotion from her childhood. She associated herself with the Dominican Order at the age of twenty and continued her life of penance, charity, and virtue.

24   St. Bartholomew, Apostle, Feast

Bartholomew, also called Nathanael, was from the town of Cana in Galilee. Jesus chose him as one the Twelve. He died a martyr's death while spreading the Gospel in India.

25 St. Louis

As king of France, Louis took his role as a Christian monarch very seriously. He strove to rule with justice and charity, giving special care to the poor. He cared for both the worldly and spiritual well-being of his subjects. He supported the Church wholeheartedly, even leading a Crusade.

St. Joseph Calasanz, Priest

Joseph Calasanz founded the Piarist order, devoted to the education of poor boys. He embraced novel educational ideas, opening public schools and befriending leading scholars of his day. He suffered great disgrace but remained faithful to the Church.

27 St. Monica, Memorial

A Christian woman married to a pagan, Monica is best known for her relationship with her son, St. Augustine. Monica devoted her tears and prayers to his conversion from his licentious ways. Ultimately, her ardent prayers bore fruit. Augustine not only converted to Christianity, he became one of its greatest bishops and theologians.

28 St. Augustine, Bishop and Doctor of the Church, Memorial

Augustine's early life of sin and excess moved his mother to constant prayer on his behalf. As an adult, he underwent a conversion experience and devoted his life to his newfound Christian faith, even becoming bishop of Hippo in Africa. Baptized by St. Ambrose in Milan, Augustine's theological writings in defense of the faith, his sermons, and especially his reflection on his life and conversion remain classics of theological thought.

29 The Passion of St. John the Baptist, Memorial

The observance recalls the martyrdom of St. John the Baptist at the hands of King Herod, spurred by Herod's fear of appearing weak in front of his court and his wife Herodias' hatred of the truth of John's preaching.

SEPTEMBER

3 *St. Gregory the Great, Pope and Doctor of the Church, Memorial*

Though beginning his religious life as a monk, Gregory's greatest achievements occurred during his papacy. He reinvigorated the Church's missionary activities, reformed the liturgy, and wrote theological works.

8 *The Nativity of the Blessed Virgin Mary, Feast*

Though not recorded in history or Scripture, this feast celebrates the birth of the Blessed Virgin Mary, nine months to the day after her Immaculate Conception.

9 *[USA] St. Peter Claver, Priest, Memorial*

After joining the Society of Jesus, Peter Claver traveled to Colombia as a missionary. There, he saw the pain and suffering endured by the slaves transported to that country. The human and spiritual needs of these slaves became the focus of Peter's ministry until his death.

12 *The Most Holy Name of Mary*

This observance calls us to recall the honor due to the name of she who bore the Only-Begotten Son of God.

13 *St. John Chrysostom, Bishop and Doctor of the Church, Memorial*

Called "Golden Mouth," John was renowned for his excellent preaching, which explained Church teaching and challenged his people to live Christian lives of devotion to the Lord. He was a good pastor to the people he served as bishop of Constantinople. His theological writings help to shape the thought of the Church even today.

14 *The Exaltation of the Holy Cross, Feast*

This feast honors the Cross of Jesus Christ, the instrument of his Death and of our salvation. On this day we recall the great love Jesus has for us, accepting death on the Cross for our salvation. This feast replaces the Mass of the day when it falls on Sunday.

15 *Our Lady of Sorrows, Memorial*

During the Presentation in the Temple of Jerusalem, Simeon warned Mary that she would face great sorrow in her life. His prediction came to pass, as her life with Christ was marked by nearly unbearable sorrow while she watched her son rejected and, ultimately, murdered by his opponents.

16 *SS. Cornelius, Pope, and Cyprian, Bishop, Martyrs, Memorial*

Cornelius and Cyprian worked together to help defend the Church from errors. Cornelius was exiled and died of the privations caused by this experience. Cyprian was martyred during the persecution of Valerian.

17 *St. Robert Bellarmine, Bishop and Doctor of the Church*

This Italian Jesuit served as a cardinal of the Church but was best known for his extensive theological writings defending the Church during the difficult time of the Counter-Reformation.

19   *St. Januarius, Bishop and Martyr*

Though little is known about his life, this bishop
of the Church was martyred during the Diocletian persecution.

**20   *SS. Andrew Kim Tae-gon, Priest, Paul Chong
Ha-sang, and Companions, Martyrs, Memorial***

Andrew Kim Tae-gen was the first Korean-born
Catholic priest. Paul Chong Ha-sang was born
into a devout Christian family that included martyrs and catechists. These men and their companions witnessed to their faith to death.

21   *St. Matthew, Apostle and Evangelist, Feast*

Matthew served as a tax collector, making him
liable to charges of corruption and collaboration
with the Roman Empire. Jesus called him to a
new life as one of the Twelve and as an Evangelist, telling the Good News of Jesus Christ.

23 St. Pius of Pietrelcina, Priest, Memorial

Often known as "Padre Pio," this Capuchin friar was known for his gifts as a confessor and spiritual director and for his willing embrace of suffering.

26 SS. Cosmas and Damian, Martyrs

Tradition recounts that these twin brothers were physicians and devout Christians. They even shared martyrdom during the Diocletian persecution.

27 St. Vincent de Paul, Priest, Memorial

This French priest is best known for his great love and compassion for the poor and his ministry to slaves who served on the galleys. He founded the Congregation of the Mission and, along with St. Louise de Marillac, the Daughters of Charity. His name lives on in the Society of St. Vincent de Paul, which attends to the needs of the poor.

28 *St. Wenceslaus, Martyr*

Wenceslaus ruled Bohemia and was noted for his just rule and his compassion for the poor, especially widows, orphans, and the imprisoned. He was assassinated in a plot instigated by his brother.

St. Lawrence Ruiz and Companions, Martyrs

Lawrence Ruiz was the first Filipino martyr. Born in Manila, he was a husband and father. He joined a Dominican missionary expedition to Japan but was arrested shortly after arrival and martyred after a year in prison. This observance commemorates the martyrs who gave their lives to bring the faith to Japan.

29 *SS. Michael, Gabriel, and Raphael,*
    Archangels, Feast

Scripture speaks of three archangels who serve
God in special ways. Michael is depicted as a
warrior, battling Satan and his minions. Gabriel
carried God's messages to Zechariah and Mary.
Raphael carried prayers to the altar of God.

30 *St. Jerome, Priest and Doctor of the*
    Church, Memorial

A student of languages, Jerome served Pope
Damasus as secretary before retiring to Bethle-
hem, where he continued to write and serve the
Church. Jerome is best known for his translation
of the Scriptures into Latin (known as the Vul-
gate) and for his Scripture commentaries.

OCTOBER

1 *St. Thérèse of the Child Jesus, Virgin and Doctor of the Church, Memorial*

As a youth, Thérèse entered the Carmelites at Lisieux and, thus, is often known as Thérèse of Lisieux or "the Little Flower." Throughout her life, she was known for her great humility and simplicity of life. The spiritual depth of her autobiographical writings earned her the title "Doctor of the Church."

2 *The Holy Guardian Angels, Memorial*

This observance honors the angels who watch over us with care throughout our lives on earth.

From its beginning until death, human life is surrounded by [the angels'] watchful care and intercession (see Mt 18:10; Lk 16:22; Ps 34:7; 91:10-13; Job 33:23-24; Zech 1:12; Tob 12:12). "Beside each believer stands an angel as protector and shepherd leading him to life" (St. Basil, *Adv. Eunomium* III, 1: PG 29, 656B). Already here on earth the Christian life shares by faith in the blessed company of angels and men united in God. (CCC, no. 336)

4   *St. Francis of Assisi, Memorial*

Born into a wealthy family, Francis eventually rejected his worldly goods and embraced a life of poverty and preaching. He founded religious orders of men and women as well as an order of laity. He strove to bring all people to love of God and neighbor and is known for his care of animals and for introducing the Christmas crèche.

6   *St. Bruno, Priest*

A highly regarded teacher of theology, Bruno declined a request to serve as a bishop. Instead, he embraced a life of solitude and penance, founding the first Carthusian monastery. Later in his life, he served as a personal adviser to Pope Urban II.

[USA] Blessed Marie Rose Durocher, Virgin

Born in Quebec, Marie Rose founded the Sisters of the Holy Names of Jesus and Mary. This religious community provided desperately needed education to the children of Canada.

7   *Our Lady of the Rosary, Memorial*

This memorial is observed on the anniversary of the Battle of Lepanto, when a fleet from several Catholic countries defeated the fleet of the Ottoman Empire, severely limiting the expansion of the Ottoman Empire in Europe. The Catholic fleet attributed their victory to the intercession of the Blessed Virgin Mary invoked through the praying of the Rosary. In the Rosary, we recall key moments in the life and ministry of Jesus Christ, reflecting ever more deeply on his Paschal Mystery.

9   *St. Denis, Bishop, and Companions, Martyrs*

Denis was the bishop of Paris, having come to the city from Italy to convert the people to Christianity. He and his companions were martyred by beheading during the Decian persecution.

St. John Leonardi, Priest

Though his first training was as a pharmacist, in his life as a priest, John Leonardi was dedicated to the religious education of young people and to the spread of the faith through the foreign missions. His work with the latter laid the foundation for the Society of the Propagation of the Faith, an organization that continues to support the Catholic missions around the world.

14   St. Callistus I, Pope and Martyr

It is believed that Callistus was a slave in his youth, eventually becoming a deacon and, ultimately, pope. As pope, he worked ardently to defend the Church's teaching. He was martyred in the early third century.

15   St. Teresa of Jesus, Virgin and Doctor of the Church, Memorial

Better known as Teresa of Avila, she worked to reform and renew the Carmelite Order of nuns, assisting in the foundation of the Discalced Carmelites. Her mystical and contemplative experiences and her writings about them are noted for their spiritual and theological depth.

16   St. Hedwig, Religious

The wife of a Polish ruler, she devoted herself to the practice of her faith and to good works throughout her life. After her husband's death, she lived in a monastery, distributing her worldly goods and living a life of prayer and penance.

St. Margaret Mary Alacoque, Virgin

Margaret Mary Alacoque was a French nun and mystic. Her mystical visions led her to promote devotion to the Sacred Heart of Jesus.

17 St. Ignatius of Antioch, Bishop and Martyr, Memorial

This bishop of Antioch was condemned to suffer martyrdom in Rome. While travelling to Rome for his execution, he wrote letters to the Christian communities along the way. These letters provide profound insight into the Church, life in Christ, and the nature of martyrdom.

18 St. Luke, Evangelist, Feast

This feast honors the writer of the Gospel of Luke and the Acts of the Apostles. Luke traveled with Paul and helped proclaim the Good News of Jesus Christ to the nations.

19 [USA] SS. John de Brébeuf and Isaac Jogues, Priests, and Companions, Martyrs, Memorial

Often called "the North American martyrs," these eight Jesuits endured brutal torture before being martyred by members of the Huron and Iroquois nations. Despite the hardships of the mission and their suffering, these martyrs retained a love of the people they served and brought to faith in Christ.

20   [USA] St. Paul of the Cross, Priest

St. Paul of the Cross founded the Congregation of the Passionists, a religious order of men who lived lives of poverty, simplicity, and harsh penance so as to meditate more fully on the Passion of the Christ. Their primary ministry was preaching to parish missions about Christ's saving Passion.

22   Blessed John Paul II, Pope

John Paul II served the Church as pope from 1978 through 2005. A skilled philosopher, poet, and playwright, as well as a theologian, he served as archbishop of Krakow, attending the Second Vatican Council in that capacity. His papacy was marked by his travels to all corners of the world, his love for youth and for the vulnerable, and his great achievements in catechesis and Church governance, particularly the publication of the *Catechism of the Catholic Church* and the *Code of Canon Law*.

23 *St. John of Capistrano, Priest*

John of Capistrano was a Franciscan friar known for his asceticism and fierce defense of the Catholic faith. At the end of his life, he led a crusade against the Ottoman Empire.

24 *St. Anthony Mary Claret, Bishop*

This Spanish priest was known for founding a religious library and a missionary order. He served as archbishop of Santiago, Cuba, where he worked ardently for the pastoral care of his people. At the end of his life, he returned to Spain and devoted his time to aiding the poor.

28 *SS. Simon and Jude, Apostles, Feast*

Little is known about these two Apostles. Scripture says that Simon came from Cana and was known as a Zealot. Jude is often called Thaddeus. Both suffered martyrs' deaths.

NOVEMBER

1 *All Saints, Solemnity*

"The custom of keeping a festival in honor of all the saints first appeared in the Churches of the East as a feast of all the martyrs whose names were known only to God" (*Holy Days*, 62). In the western Church, this solemnity was originally celebrated in May, but the date was changed in the eighth century, following the English custom, which likely had originated in Ireland (see *Holy Days*, 64). On this solemnity, we recall the holy men and women who, having completed their earthly journeys, now live forever with God. These saints, though not canonized, offer us models of abiding faith and love of God and neighbor. This solemnity replaces the Mass of the day when it falls on Sunday. While this solemnity does not have a proper vigil Mass, its vigil day is widely observed as All Hallow's Eve—Halloween.

2   The Commemoration of All the Faithful Departed (All Souls' Day)

Closely related to the Solemnity of All Saints is the Commemoration of All the Faithful Departed, commonly called All Souls' Day. On this day, we remember all the departed, praying that, through the mercy of God, they may come to dwell in the Heavenly Kingdom. This commemoration originated at the monastery of Cluny in the eleventh century and spread among Benedictine monasteries. It was added to the general church calendar in the fourteenth century (*Holy Days*, 67-68). This commemoration replaces the Mass of the day when it falls on Sunday.

3   St. Martin de Porres, Religious

Martin was born in Lima, Peru, of mixed-race parents. He suffered much discrimination because of his birth but overcame it by reflecting the love of Christ. He has become a patron saint for persons of mixed race. As a Dominican brother, he was widely known for his care for the poor and sick and his deep love for the Eucharist.

4   *St. Charles Borromeo, Bishop, Memorial*

As cardinal archbishop of Milan, Charles Borromeo worked incessantly to encourage the priests and people of his diocese to live faithful lives. He established seminaries to ensure the proper training of priests and introduced reforms where practice of the faith had grown lax.

9   *The Dedication of the Lateran Basilica, Feast*

The Basilica of St. John Lateran Hill in Rome is the cathedral church of the Bishop of Rome, the pope. As such, it is considered the mother church of the whole Catholic Church. This feast is celebrated throughout the Latin Church as a sign of the whole Church's unity with the Holy Father. It replaces the Mass of the day when it falls on Sunday.

10   *St. Leo the Great, Pope and Doctor of the Church, Memorial*

Leo the Great served the Church as pope in the fifth century. In his sermons, he preached the faith with great passion and integrity. He defended the faith against errors and increased the unity of the Church while helping to protect it from the barbarian invasions.

11 St. Martin of Tours, Bishop, Memorial

Martin of Tours gave up his life as a soldier to embrace the Christian faith. He lived as monk before becoming bishop of Tours in France. He was known for his pastoral care of his people and his great generosity to the poor.

12 St. Josaphat, Bishop and Martyr, Memorial

Josaphat was a bishop of the Church in Ukraine. He sought ardently to improve the education of priests and the unity of the Church. He was martyred by an axe-blow.

13 [USA] St. Frances Xavier Cabrini, Virgin, Memorial

Often called "Mother Cabrini," Frances Xavier Cabrini was the first U.S. citizen to become a saint. She immigrated to the United States in 1889 to serve the growing immigrant population. She and her sisters founded many social service institutions, including hospitals and orphanages.

15 St. Albert the Great, Bishop and Doctor of the Church

Albert the Great was both a great theologian and a great scholar, showing the compatibility of faith and reason. His works discussed faith, philosophy, and the sciences. Thomas Aquinas is counted among his students.

16 St. Margaret of Scotland

As the wife and mother of kings of Scotland, Margaret used her position to promote religious practice and unity. She encouraged just rule and engaged in works of charity to assist the poor.

St. Gertrude, Virgin

In her first years as a nun, Gertrude studied literature and philosophy, later turning her attention to spirituality and theology. She experienced mystical visions of Jesus' divine love.

17 St. Elizabeth of Hungary, Religious, Memorial

With the consent of her ruler husband, Elizabeth spent much of her married life providing for the needs of the poor. After his death, she divested herself of her possessions and lived a life of prayer and poverty, attending to the sick in a hospital she had established.

18 The Dedication of the Basilicas of SS. Peter and Paul, Apostles

This observance celebrates the dedications of the Roman churches named for SS. Peter and Paul. It provides an opportunity to reflect on the important role played by these apostles in spreading the Word of God and ensuring the unity of the Church.

[USA] St. Rose Philippine Duchesne, Virgin

A sister of the Society of the Sacred Heart, this French woman spent much of her life serving in the midwestern states of the United States. Devoted to her ministry of education, she was renowned for her strong prayer life.

21 The Presentation of the Blessed Virgin Mary, Memorial

Though the date of this memorial is tied to the dedication of a church to Mary built near the site of the Jerusalem Temple, it commemorates Mary's presentation to the Lord in the Temple.

22 St. Cecilia, Virgin and Martyr, Memorial

Though many legends exist about St. Cecilia, little is known of her life apart from the fact that she suffered martyrdom in the early centuries of the Church. Mentioned by name in the Roman Canon (Eucharistic Prayer I), she is best known as the patron saint of musicians.

23 St. Clement I, Pope and Martyr

Clement was one of the first Bishops of Rome and, thus, one of the first popes. His letter to the Corinthians is one of the earliest non-biblical Church writings. This letter stressed the importance of unity in the Church under the governance of bishops and presbyters.

St. Columban, Abbot

This Irish missionary founded monasteries throughout Europe. He was especially devoted to penance for the forgiveness of sins.

[USA] Blessed Miguel Agustín Pro, Priest and Martyr

This Mexican Jesuit priest served the Church in his home country during a period of intense anti-clericalism. During a portion of his priesthood, he was forced to minister in an underground church. For his continued service as a priest in violation of the government, he was executed without a trial.

24   *St. Andrew Dũng-Lạc, Priest, and Companions, Martyrs, Memorial*

Andrew and his 107 companions, both priests and laity, were martyred in Vietnam in the seventeenth through nineteenth centuries. Through their preaching, lives of faith, and witness unto death, they strengthened the Church in Vietnam.

25   *St. Catherine of Alexandria, Virgin and Martyr*

Martyred in the early part of the fourth century, Catherine was known for her intelligence, her deep faith, and the power of her intercession.

30 *St. Andrew, Apostle, Feast*

Andrew was the brother of Peter and one of the Twelve Apostles. Originally a disciple of John the Baptist, the Gospel of John records that he brought Peter to Christ. In other places as well, the Gospel recounts that he brought people to Christ, a task he continued with his preaching after the Resurrection.

Last Sunday in Ordinary Time: Our Lord Jesus Christ, King of the Universe, Solemnity

For this observance, see the discussion under "Ordinary Time" (pp. 37-48).

Fourth Thursday: [USA] **Thanksgiving Day**

The dioceses of the United States may use proper orations and a proper Preface when celebrating this national commemoration of gratitude for all God's gifts.

DECEMBER

3 *St. Francis Xavier, Priest, Memorial*

One of the first members of the Society of Jesus, Francis Xavier traveled to India, Indonesia, and Japan to preach the Gospel and bring people to the Catholic faith.

4 *St. John Damascene, Priest and Doctor of the Church*

Born in Damascus, John spent much of his life in a monastery. He wrote many hymns as well as theological works about the Assumption of Mary and defending the use of holy images.

6 *St. Nicholas, Bishop*

This bishop of Myra in Turkey was renowned for his abundant generosity to the poor. His generosity was typically expressed through the giving of gifts.

7 *St. Ambrose, Bishop and Doctor of the Church, Memorial*

This archbishop of Milan was one of the great theologians of his day, composing masterworks on the sacraments, Scripture, and other doctrinal matters. He was known for his skill as a pastor and for his love and care for the poor.

8 *[USA] The Immaculate Conception of the Blessed Virgin Mary (Patronal Feastday of the United States of America), Solemnity*

This solemnity celebrates Mary's conception in her mother's womb without the stain of Original Sin. As such, it speaks to God's plan for salvation, preparing the one who would become the Mother of his Only-Begotten Son.

This feast was celebrated in some monasteries before the beginning of the eighth century and became widespread in the eighteenth century. In the United States, celebration of this observance predates the Declaration of Independence. The bishops commended the nation to the patronage of Mary under the title of the Immaculate Conception in 1846. It became a nationwide holy day in 1885 (see *Holy Days*, 74-75).

9   *St. Juan Diego Cuauhtlatoatzin*

Juan Diego was an indigenous Mexican who converted to Christianity at age fifty. A few years later, he had several visions of the Blessed Virgin and carried her messages to the bishop. The Blessed Virgin's image appeared on the tilma (cloak) he was wearing.

11   *St. Damasus I, Pope*

This fourth-century pope worked tirelessly to resolve schisms in the Church and to defend the Church's teaching against error. He had a particular devotion to the martyrs and left inscriptions on many of their tombs.

12   *[USA] Our Lady of Guadalupe, Feast*

The Blessed Virgin Mary appeared to Juan Diego and left him with her image imprinted on his tilma (cloak). Her messages were filled with love and compassion for the people. Our Lady of Guadalupe is the patroness of the Americas.

13   *St. Lucy, Virgin and Martyr, Memorial*

Lucy suffered martyrdom during the Diocletian persecution. Mentioned by name in the Roman Canon (Eucharistic Prayer I), she is best known as the patron saint of the blind.

14 *St. John of the Cross, Priest and Doctor of the Church, Memorial*

One of the founders of the Discalced Carmelites, John of the Cross led a reform of the Carmelite Order despite much struggle. His poetry and mystical writings give evidence of his deep spirituality and compassion.

21 *St. Peter Canisius, Priest and Doctor of the Church*

This Jesuit priest traveled from Holland to Germany to preach in support of the Catholic faith. His catechetical writings offered accessible explanations of the truths of the faith to the laity.

23 *St. John of Kanty, Priest*

This Polish priest was known for his scholarship in theology and science as well as for his pastoral care. His personal devotion and humility were examples to all who knew him.

25 *The Nativity of the Lord (Christmas), Solemnity*

26 *St. Stephen, the First Martyr, Feast*

27 St. John, Apostle and Evangelist, Feast

28 The Holy Innocents, Martyrs, Feast

For these observances, see the discussion under "Christmas" (pp. 12-17).

29 St. Thomas Becket, Bishop and Martyr

Previously chancellor of England, as the archbishop of Canterbury, Thomas Becket defended the Church's rights against the encroachment of the king. He was murdered in his cathedral in Canterbury.

31 St. Sylvester I, Pope

Sylvester served as pope in the first part of the fourth century, a time of great discord in the Church, as various heresies and schisms threatened the Church's unity.

Sunday within the Octave of the Nativity, or, if there is no Sunday, December 30: The Holy Family of Jesus, Mary, and Joseph, Feast

For this observance, see the discussion under "Christmas" (pp. 12-17).

Appendix

At the time of publication, the dioceses of the United States were awaiting Holy See confirmation of the following addition to the calendar.

January 23: St. Marianne Cope, Virgin
Marianne Cope entered the Sisters of St. Francis in Syracuse, New York, and assisted in caring for the sick and for immigrants. In 1883, she traveled to Molokai, Hawaii, to care for lepers in a home she established.

IV. SPECIAL
OBSERVANCES

n addition to the liturgical seasons and saints' days, popular piety has dedicated certain days and months to certain religious observances. Many of these observances are closely related to the liturgical calendar; however, it is important that these popular celebrations not overshadow the liturgical seasons and Sundays.

In some places, the month of March is a time of particular devotion to St. Joseph.

Popular piety dedicates the month of May to the Blessed Virgin Mary. In some places, images of Mary are crowned with flowers. To keep this piety from obscuring the celebration of the Easter season,

> the pious exercises practiced at this time could emphasize Our Lady's participation in the Paschal mystery (see Jn 19:25-27), and the Pentecost event (see Acts 1:14) with which the Church begins: Our Lady journeys with the Church having shared in the novum of the Resurrection, under the guidance of the Holy Spirit. The fifty days are also a time for the celebration of the sacraments of Christian initiation and of the mystagogy. The

pious exercises connected with the month of May could easily highlight the earthly role played by the glorified Queen of Heaven, here and now, in the celebration of the Sacraments of Baptism, Confirmation and Holy Eucharist [see Congregation for Divine Worship, Circular Letter, *Guidelines and proposals for the celebration of the Marian Year*, 25-31]. (*Directory*, no. 191)

In addition, Saturdays are dedicated to Mary. Any Saturday in Ordinary Time that does not have a proper celebration may be celebrated as an optional memorial of the Blessed Virgin. These optional memorials provide

a remembrance of the maternal example and discipleship of the Blessed Virgin Mary who, strengthened by faith and hope, on that great Saturday on which Our Lord lay in the tomb, was the only one of the disciples to hold vigil in expectation of the Lord's resurrection; it is a prelude and introduction to the celebration of Sunday, the weekly memorial of the Resurrection of Christ; it is a sign that the Virgin Mary is continuously present and operative in the life of the Church. (Congregation for Divine Worship, Circular Letter, *Guidelines and Proposals for the Celebration of the Marian Year*, no. 5 in *Directory* no. 188)

During the month of June (the month of the Solemnity of the Sacred Heart) and on First Fridays, many Catholics maintain a devotion to the Sacred Heart, recalling the divine love that pours forth from the heart of Jesus. This devotion typically focuses on participation in the Sacraments of Penance and Eucharist. "Devotion to the Sacred Heart is a wonderful historical expression of the Church's piety for Christ, her Spouse and Lord: it calls for a fundamental attitude of conversion and reparation, of love and gratitude, apostolic commitment and dedication to Christ and his saving work" (*Directory*, no. 172).

Since October includes the Memorial of Our Lady of the Rosary, it is unsurprising that popular piety gives special attention to the Rosary during this month. This is an excellent opportunity for a liturgical blessing of rosaries (see the *Book of Blessings*, Chapter 45) and communal recitation of the Rosary with meditation on Christ's Paschal Mystery.

Since November begins with commemorations of All Saints and All Souls, it is not surprising that popular piety during this month centers around the four last things: death, judgment, heaven, and hell. Some dioceses hold special Masses in Catholic cemeteries. Parishes hold special memorial services using the Office for the Dead. Families visit cemeteries to recall deceased family members and other loved ones.

The faithful are inspired to model their lives after the saints and to pray ardently for the souls in purgatory.

A Conference of Bishops may establish Rogation and Ember Days as days of special prayers. "The Church is accustomed to entreat the Lord for the various needs of humanity, especially for the fruits of the earth and for human labor, and to give thanks to him publicly" (*Norms*, no. 45).

In addition to the seasons and saints, the Holy See and the USCCB have highlighted certain periods of each year to pray for and study particular concerns. The observances established by the Holy See include the Week of Prayer for Christian Unity (the week surrounding January 25), World Day for Consecrated Life (February 2), World Day for the Sick (February 11), World Day for Communications (Sunday before Pentecost), World Youth Day (Palm Sunday, unless there is an international celebration), and World Mission Sunday (next to last Sunday in October). The observances established by the USCCB include National Migration Week (the week following Epiphany), Catholic Schools Week (beginning the last

Sunday in January), Catechetical Sunday (third Sunday in September), and Respect Life Month (October). These observances might be handled well in the homily or the General Intercessions or by including a blessing in accord with the approved rite in the *Book of Blessings*. In no instance should these observances overshadow the liturgical calendar or the Sunday celebration.

V. CONCLUSION

"Recalling thus the mysteries of redemption, the Church opens to the faithful the riches of her Lord's powers and merits, so that these are in some way made present for all time, and the faithful are enabled to lay hold upon them and become filled with saving grace" (*Constitution on the Sacred Liturgy*, no. 102).

The purpose of the liturgical calendar and all liturgical celebrations is to draw the faithful ever more deeply into the Paschal Mystery of Jesus Christ so that, when our time on earth is ended, we may share forever in the banquet of the Lamb.

Acknowledgments

Cover illustration and title page, *The Good Shepherd*, detail from the Chapel of the Good Shepherd. Bancel La Farge and Ravenna Mosaic Company, 1926. Photograph courtesy of the Basilica of the National Shrine of the Immaculate Conception, Washington, DC, 2011. Photographer: Geraldine M. Rohling.

p. 9, "The Prophet Isaiah," detail from *The Birth of Jesus*, Chapel of the Joyful Mysteries of the Rosary. Joseph L. Youngand Ravenna Mosaic Company, 1967. Photograph courtesy of the Basilica of the National Shrine of the Immaculate Conception, Washington, DC, 2011. Photographer: Geraldine M. Rohling.

p. 10, "The Incarnation" scene, *The Incarnation*. Knights of Columbus dome mosaic. Leandro Miguel Velasco and Travisanutto Mosaics, Italy, 2007. Photograph courtesy of the Basilica of the National Shrine of the Immaculate Conception, Washington, DC, 2007. Photographer: Geraldine M. Rohling.

p. 13, "Adoration of the Magi," detail from *The Birth of Jesus*. Chapel of the Joyful Mysteries of the Rosary. Joseph L. Young and Ravenna Mosaic Company, 1967. Photograph courtesy of the Basilica of the National Shrine of the Immaculate Conception, Washington, DC, 2011. Photographer: Geraldine M. Rohling.

p. 20, "Jesus' Entry into Jerusalem." Detail of stained glass window, South Bay 9, Cathedral of Mary our Queen, Baltimore, Maryland © 2009 Terry Ann Modica of Catholic Digital Resources, *catholicdr.com*. All rights reserved.

p. 23, *The Lord's Supper*, Chapel of the Blessed Sacrament. Millard Owen Sheets and Ravenna Mosaic Company, St. Louis, 1970. Photograph Courtesy of the Basilica of the National Shrine of the Immaculate Conception, Washington, DC, 2007. Photographer: Geraldine M. Rohling.

p. 24, "The Crucifixion" detail from the *Blessed Sacrament* mosaic by Millard Owen Sheets and the Ravenna Mosaic Company, 1970. Photograph courtesy of the Basilica of the National Shrine of the Immaculate Conception, Washington, DC, 2011. Photographer: Geraldine M. Rohling.

p. 29, *The Resurrection*. Chapel of the Glorious Mysteries of the Rosary. John de Rosen and Peter Recker, Germany, 1960. Photograph courtesy of the Basilica of the National Shrine of the Immaculate Conception, Washington, DC, 2011. Photographer: Geraldine M. Rohling.

p. 32, *The Ascension*. Detail from the Upper Sacristy fresco by Leandro Miguel Velasco, 1967. Photograph courtesy of the Basilica of the National Shrine of the Immaculate Conception, Washington, DC, 2009. Photographer: Geraldine M. Rohling.

p. 35, *The Descent of the Holy Spirit*. Baldachin altar, interior dome, bronze and mosaic by George Snowden, 1960. Photograph courtesy of the Basilica of the National Shrine of the Immaculate Conception, Washington, DC, 2005. Photographer: Geraldine M. Rohling.

p. 36, "Jesus" detail from *The Ascension of Jesus*, Chapel of the Glorious Mysteries of the Rosary. John de Rosen and Peter Recker, Germany, 1960. Photograph courtesy of the Basilica of the National Shrine of the Immaculate Conception, Washington, DC, 2006. Photographer: Geraldine M. Rohling.

p. 53, *Fractio panis*. Mary Chase Stratton, 1927. Based on the fresco of the 2nd century in the Greek Chapel in the catacomb of Priscilla. Photograph courtesy of the Basilica of the National Shrine of the Immaculate Conception, Washington, DC, 2011. Photographer: Geraldine M. Rohling.

p. 54, *St. Joseph, the Defender of the Faith and the Patron of Workers*. Austin J. Purves, Jr. and Venetian Art Mosaics Studios, 1967. Photograph courtesy of the Basilica of the National Shrine of the Immaculate Conception, Washington, DC, 2007. Photographer: Robert Isacson.

p. 57, *The Annunciation*. Chapel of the Joyful Mysteries of the Rosary. Joseph L. Young and Ravenna Mosaic Company, 1967. Photograph courtesy of the Basilica of the National Shrine of the Immaculate Conception, Washington, DC, 2011. Photographer: Geraldine M. Rohling.

p. 72, *Petrus, Paulus*. Mary Chase Stratton, 1927. Photograph courtesy of the Basilica of the National Shrine of the Immaculate Conception, Washington, DC, 2010. Photographer: Geraldine M. Rohling.

p. 85, *The Transfiguration*. Luminous Mysteries, Chapel of Our Lady of Pompeii. Leandro Miguel Velasco and Travisanutto Mosaics, Italy, 2008. Photograph courtesy of the Basilica of the National Shrine of the Immaculate Conception, Washington, DC, 2011. Photographer: Geraldine M. Rohling.

p. 88, *The Assumption*. Chapel of the Glorious Mysteries of the Rosary. John de Rosen and Peter Recker, Germany, 1960. Photograph courtesy of the Basilica of the National Shrine of the Immaculate Conception, Washington, DC, 2011. Photographer: Geraldine M. Rohling.

p. 101, "Gabriel the Archangel" detail from "The Annunciation" scene, *The Incarnation*. Knights of Columbus dome mosaic. Leandro Miguel Velasco and Travisanutto Mosaics, Italy, 2007. Photograph courtesy of the Basilica of the National Shrine of the Immaculate Conception, Washington, DC, 2011. Photographer: Geraldine M. Rohling.

p. 110, "All Saints" detail from *The Last Judgment*. Mary Reardon and Ravenna Mosaic Company, 1973. Photograph courtesy of the Basilica of the National Shrine of the Immaculate Conception, Washington, DC, 2011. Photographer: Geraldine M. Rohling.

p. 121, *The Immaculate Conception*. Mosaic reproduction of *La Purissma Bionda* by Bartolomé Estaban Murillo manufactured by the Reverenda Fabbrica di San Pietro di Vaticano (RFSPV), 1930. Photograph courtesy of the Basilica of the National Shrine of the Immaculate Conception, Washington, DC, 2009.

p. 122, *Our Lady of Guadalupe*. Mary Reardon and Ravenna Mosaic Company, 1967. Photograph courtesy of the Basilica of the National Shrine of the Immaculate Conception, Washington, DC, 2004. Photographer: John Whitman.

p. 133, "The Resurrection" scene detail, The Redemption. Leandro Miguel Velasco and Travisanutto Mosaics, Italy, 2006. Photograph courtesy of the Basilica of the National Shrine of the Immaculate Conception, Washington, DC, 2011. Photographer: Geraldine M. Rohling.